I0446344

Published by Rafal Laba Content

For permission requests, write to the publisher at: rafal@rafallaba.pl

First Edition, November 2023

This second edition, January 2024

The information in this book is meant to supplement, not replace, job search strategies and techniques. While all attempts have been made to verify information provided in this publication, neither the author nor the publisher assumes any responsibility for errors, omissions, or contrary interpretations of the subject matter herein. This book is provided with the understanding that the publisher and author are not engaged in rendering legal, accounting, or other professional services. If legal advice or other expert assistance is required, the services of a competent professional should be sought.

Table of Content

How to Read This Book 4

Brief Overview 5

My Experience..7

Chapter 1: Understanding the Job Market 9

    Current Trends: 9

    Identifying Opportunities: 12

Chapter 2: Crafting a Winning LinkedIn Profile 15

    Profile Basics: Mastering Your LinkedIn Presence..........15

    Advanced Tips: Making Your Profile Stand Out Using AI Tools for
Optimization 19

Chapter 3: Resume and Cover Letter Mastery.......................23

    Resume Writing: Step-by-step Guidance 23

    Cover Letter Creation: Tips for Writing Compelling Cover Letters
That Complement Your Resume 34

Chapter 4: Evaluating Job Opportunities................................41

Chapter 5: Enhanced Interview Preparation Strategies 51

Chapter 6: Salary Negotiation and Benefits...........................61

Chapter 7: Using AI and Open-Source Tools Effectively 70

Chapter 8: Maximizing Networking in Your Job Search........75

Chapter 9: Maintaining a Log of Your Job Seeking Activities...........84

Conclusion 88

Appendix 92

How to Read This Book

"Your Path to Employment" is a comprehensive guide designed to be flexible and adaptable to your unique job search journey. Whether you are a first-time job seeker, a seasoned professional contemplating a career change, or someone re-entering the workforce, this book caters to a wide array of needs and backgrounds.

You can choose to read this book from beginning to end to gain a holistic understanding of the modern job market and how to navigate it using AI and open-source tools. Each chapter builds upon the previous, offering a structured and methodical approach to job hunting, from understanding market trends to mastering interview techniques and negotiating salaries.

Alternatively, you can dive into specific chapters or sections that are most relevant to your current needs. For instance, if you're focusing on enhancing your LinkedIn profile, Chapter 2 provides detailed insights and advanced tips specifically for this purpose. Or, if you're preparing for interviews, Chapter 5 offers targeted strategies and AI-powered mock interview scenarios to sharpen your skills.

A unique feature of this book is the inclusion of 210 AI prompts, strategically placed throughout the chapters. These prompts serve as practical tools to leverage AI in various aspects of your job search, such as crafting compelling resumes, preparing for interviews, and enhancing your LinkedIn profile. These AI prompts are designed to provide you with hands-on, practical assistance, making your job search process more efficient and effective.

Remember, the journey of job hunting is dynamic and often requires an adaptable approach. This book is intended to be a resource you can return to time and again, offering guidance, insights, and practical tools at every stage of your job search. Embrace the journey, utilize the resources at your disposal, and step confidently towards your career goals.

Brief Overview

Welcome to "Your Path to Employment". A Guide to Navigating Job Markets with AI and Open-Source Tools. This e-book is designed to be your companion and guide in the often challenging journey of job hunting. In today's rapidly evolving job market, where technology plays a significant role, understanding how to leverage digital tools effectively can make a substantial difference in your job search.

The aim of this guide is twofold. First, it seeks to demystify the process of finding and securing a job in the modern digital landscape. Whether you're a recent graduate, a professional seeking a career change, or re-entering the workforce, this book provides practical advice, step-by-step guides, and insider knowledge to enhance your job search.

Second, and perhaps more importantly, this e-book introduces you to the world of AI and open-source tools that can significantly augment your job search efforts. From optimizing your LinkedIn profile using AI algorithms to preparing for interviews with AI-powered mock sessions, we will explore how these technologies can give you an edge.

The content is crafted with simplicity and clarity in mind, ensuring it is accessible to job seekers of various backgrounds, including those for whom English is not a first language. Each chapter is structured to not only provide you with essential knowledge but also to empower you to apply these insights practically.

As we delve into the chapters, you will learn how to navigate job listing platforms, create compelling resumes and cover letters, evaluate job opportunities, prepare for interviews, leverage your personal network and negotiate salaries effectively. Additionally, we'll explore how to utilize AI tools like ChatGPT, Bing, and Bard in your job search process, emphasizing free or open-source options to ensure affordability.

By the end of this e-book, you will be equipped with the knowledge, skills, and tools to navigate the job market confidently and effectively. So, let's embark on this journey together, paving the way towards your successful career.

As you embark on the insightful journey this book offers, remember that it's not just a source of guidance but a significant time-saver. By distilling years of expertise, cutting-edge techniques, and invaluable tools into one comprehensive guide, 'Your Fast Path to Employment' saves you weeks, even months, of research and trial-and-error. This book is your condensed roadmap of experiences and strategies, empowering you to navigate the job market with efficiency and confidence.

My Experience

In this section, I draw from my extensive professional journey, marked by resilience, adaptability, and success in the dynamic world of sales and people management. My career, spanning over 25 years, has been a testament to my dedication and skill in navigating the ever-changing business landscape.

Consistent Career Stability: For more than two decades, I maintained a steady and uninterrupted career path, a reflection of my ability to adapt, lead and deliver results. My tenure in various high-responsibility roles in the IT industry, including managerial and directorial positions at prominent companies like Oracle, Avaya, Motorola and OpenText, has equipped me with a deep understanding of sales strategies, team leadership, and business development across diverse worldwide markets.

Proven Leadership in Talent Acquisition: A significant aspect of my career has been the successful recruitment and development of talented individuals. I have hired dozens of professionals, nurturing their growth and steering them towards achieving their personal and professional goals. This experience has not only honed my eye for talent but also deepened my understanding of what makes a candidate stand out in the job market.

Resilience in Adversity: Despite an impressive track record of never losing a job for over a quarter of a century, I faced unemployment twice in my fifties. These instances tested my resilience and adaptability. However, drawing on my extensive experience and professional network, I successfully navigated these challenges, securing new positions within two months each time. This part of my journey is particularly significant as it underscores the importance of perseverance, networking, and staying abreast of industry trends, especially in times of uncertainty.

Diverse Skill Set and Continuous Learning: My career is also marked by a commitment to continuous learning and skill enhancement. From completing rigorous programs at the Mentoring and Coaching Academy to acquiring certifications in Blockchain and Cryptocurrency, I have consistently expanded my knowledge base. This dedication to learning has been crucial in keeping my skills relevant and has allowed me to adapt swiftly to market changes.

In sharing these experiences, I aim to provide readers with not just a glimpse into my professional journey, but also valuable insights and lessons that can be applied in their own career paths. My story is one of persistence, adaptability, and the constant pursuit of growth, all of which are essential in today's fast-paced and ever-evolving job market.

Chapter 1: Understanding the Job Market

Current Trends:

In today's rapidly evolving job market, staying informed about current trends has never been more crucial. These trends are shaped by various factors: technological advancements, economic shifts, and cultural changes. Each plays a vital role in molding the employment landscape. It's essential to note that the pace of change in the job market has accelerated dramatically. Changes that used to unfold over years can now transpire within months. Some shifts have been hastened by force majeure events, such as the Pandemic, while others are propelled by rapid technological progress. As a result, your work situation could change overnight, often without significant or visible warning signs.

Reflecting on my own experiences, I recall the first major layoff in my professional life. It was the early 2000s, and I was working at Lucent Technologies, a company that no longer exists. I was supervising a technical team then. We were tasked with reducing staff, and it took the local management team over six months to prepare and execute these changes. Today, such a timeframe could be condensed to a mere six days, and I wouldn't be surprised if it soon shrinks to just six hours. The lesson here is that your employment situation can change rapidly, and you should be prepared. Thinking ahead is essential, so you're not caught off guard.

This topic might well be a subject for another book, but what I'd like to suggest is that preparation is key. If you're not actively job-hunting right now, reading this book is a form of preparation. I also advise being ready for changes from both a mental and financial perspective. Maintaining at least six months of savings can help secure your position in unexpected situations. For now, let's delve into the current trends shaping the evolving job market.

Rise of Remote Work:

The remote work trend, significantly accelerated by the COVID-19 pandemic, has reshaped the traditional workplace. Companies are increasingly adopting hybrid or fully remote models, allowing employees to work from anywhere. This shift not only enhances work-life balance but also opens job opportunities across global markets, making talent acquisition more diverse.

Technology and Automation:

The integration of AI, machine learning, and automation is revolutionizing various sectors. This transformation is not only creating new job roles but also redefining existing ones. It underscores the growing importance of digital literacy, technological proficiency, and adaptability in the modern workplace. Continuous learning and upskilling in these areas are becoming essential for career progression.

Focus on Green Jobs:

With heightened awareness of environmental issues, there's been a surge in demand for 'green jobs'. These roles, spanning from renewable energy to environmental conservation and sustainable business practices, are at the forefront of combating climate change. They offer opportunities for those passionate about making a positive environmental impact through their work.

Healthcare and Wellness:

The healthcare sector, already a significant part of the economy, has experienced further growth due to an aging population and a renewed focus on health and wellness in the post-pandemic era. This trend has not only increased demand for traditional healthcare roles but also for positions in mental health, wellness, and alternative medicine.

Gig Economy Expansion:

The gig economy, characterized by flexible, freelance, and contract-based roles, continues to grow. It offers an alternative to traditional employment, appealing to those seeking greater flexibility, autonomy, and a variety of work experiences. This trend is reshaping career trajectories and how people view job security and career development.

Skills Over Degrees:

There's a noticeable shift in employers prioritizing skills and practical experience over formal education. This change benefits non-traditional candidates who have acquired their expertise through online courses, bootcamps, self-teaching, or work experience. It highlights the importance of skill-based hiring and continuous personal development.

Emphasis on Workplace Diversity and Inclusion:

There is an increasing focus on creating diverse and inclusive work environments. Companies are recognizing the value of diverse perspectives and experiences in driving innovation and growth. This trend is leading to more inclusive hiring practices and workplace policies.

Mental Health Awareness:

Mental health is becoming a priority in the workplace. Companies are increasingly offering resources and support for employee mental health and well-being, recognizing its impact on productivity and employee retention.

By understanding and adapting to these trends, job seekers can better position themselves in the market, aligning their skills and experiences with the evolving demands of the modern workplace. This knowledge not only helps in targeting suitable job opportunities but also in shaping one's career development in a way that's aligned with future job market trends.

Identifying Opportunities:

Finding job opportunities in today's dynamic market demands a strategic approach and effective use of digital platforms. It's important to recognize that no single tool or platform guarantees success. However, being aware of and knowledgeable about various services can significantly boost your chances. Different tools may work better for different individuals in various locations, and some might become irrelevant for your specific needs. Therefore, it's crucial to explore these tools thoroughly, assess their utility, and determine what works best for you.

From my personal experience, I've found that personal relationships are incredibly effective. Maintaining positive and authentic connections with colleagues at work, as well as with people in your personal life, is extremely important. But it's equally crucial to utilize tools and technology to nurture these relationships and support your job search process. For instance, even if you can reach out to a college friend who is now a CEO, you still need to present yourself professionally. This means sending a well-crafted CV, having a strong LinkedIn profile, conducting professional job interviews, and demonstrating your readiness. You should be able to talk not only about your competencies but also about your potential employer's needs and vision.

This is why the tools and technologies discussed below are essential in your path to successful employment. I believe that only a combination of all these techniques can lead to success in your job-seeking endeavors.

Leveraging LinkedIn[1]: LinkedIn is a multifaceted platform, offering job listings, networking opportunities, and a wealth of industry knowledge.

Ensure your profile is complete and actively engage with content and groups in your field to boost visibility.

Utilizing Glassdoor[2]: Glassdoor is an invaluable resource for gaining insights into company cultures, salary benchmarks, and interview expectations. Tailor your applications based on this information and set up alerts for jobs that align with your career goals.

Exploring Indeed[3]: As a comprehensive aggregator of job listings, Indeed is essential for a broad job search. Customize your search criteria and take advantage of the easy application process by uploading your resume.

Niche Job Boards and Forums: For specific industries, niche job boards can be a goldmine. These platforms often list specialized roles that are not widely advertised on larger job sites.

Company Websites and Career Pages: Directly visiting company career pages can reveal opportunities not yet listed elsewhere. Make a habit of checking the websites of your target companies.

Networking and Referrals: Build your network through industry events, webinars, and workshops. Personal referrals can dramatically enhance your job prospects.

Social Media Platforms: X (Twitter), Facebook, and even Instagram can be unexpectedly rich sources for job opportunities. Follow and engage with industry leaders and relevant company accounts.

Headhunters and Recruitment Agencies: Professional recruiters and headhunters can be pivotal in your job search. Companies like Robert Half[4], Korn Ferry[5], and Spencer Stuart[6] specialize in matching candidates with suitable roles. It's beneficial to explore local

---

[1] https://www.linkedin.com/
[2] https://www.glassdoor.com/
[3] https://www.indeed.com/
[4] https://www.roberthalf.com/
[5] https://www.kornferry.com/
[6] https://www.spencerstuart.com/

headhunting firms and individual recruiters as well, as they often have a deeper understanding of the local job market and might prove more effective in certain cases.

Don't hesitate to ask friends and family for recommendations and contacts. Utilize platforms like LinkedIn and other social media to reach out for contacts and opinions. Engaging with industry leaders and relevant company accounts on these platforms can also provide valuable insights and connections. Remember, the more you network and gather information, the better your chances of finding suitable job opportunities.

Alternative Professional Platforms: Sites like Xing[7] and AngelList[8] offer unique networking and job search opportunities, particularly in specific regions or sectors.

Stay Informed and Be Proactive: Keep abreast of industry trends and tailor your skills and resume to meet the evolving demands of your target sector.

In conclusion, a strategic approach to job searching, utilizing a mix of digital platforms, personal networking, and the services of professional recruiters, is crucial. By leveraging these varied resources and staying adaptable, you can navigate the job market successfully and find opportunities that align with your career aspirations.

---

[7] https://www.xing.com/
[8] https://angel.co/

Chapter 2: Crafting a Winning LinkedIn Profile

Profile Basics: Mastering Your LinkedIn Presence

There are varied opinions about LinkedIn and its effectiveness in the job search process. Some argue that applying for jobs through LinkedIn is largely futile, citing a mere 2.5% chance of success. Indeed, it's not uncommon to see over a thousand applicants for a job posted just a day earlier, which significantly diminishes one's chances of even securing an interview. While these points are valid, I believe LinkedIn's true value lies elsewhere.

A professional LinkedIn profile serves as your virtual business card or resume. In my experience, on several occasions when I applied for jobs outside of LinkedIn, my profile was later visited by multiple individuals from the hiring company during various stages of the recruitment process. In two instances, these visits ultimately led to job offers. This illustrates that while the direct application success rate may be low, LinkedIn plays a crucial role in providing a comprehensive professional snapshot to potential employers.

Your LinkedIn profile is your digital front door to the professional world. It's not just an online resume; it's a platform for personal branding, networking, and often the first impression you make on potential employers. Here's how to optimize your profile for maximum impact:

Professional Profile Picture[9]:

A clear, professional headshot is essential. Choose a photo with good lighting and a neutral background. Dress professionally, similar to how you would for an interview. Avoid casual or group photos. You might use AI tools like Canva[10] or Remove.bg[11] to optimize your business photo

Remember, this photo sets the tone for your professional image online.

Compelling Headline:

Your LinkedIn headline should encapsulate your professional essence. It's more than just a job title; it's a concise declaration of your expertise and the unique value you bring to the table. To maximize your visibility in searches, it's crucial to incorporate keywords that are relevant to your industry. These keywords help you appear in search results when potential employers or connections are looking for professionals with your skills and experience.

Consider using an AI tool or prompt to assist in crafting your headline. Such tools can help you identify and integrate the most impactful keywords, ensuring that your headline is not only reflective of your professional identity but also optimized for LinkedIn's search algorithms. Remember, a well-crafted headline can make a significant difference in how you are perceived and discovered in the professional world.

Engaging Summary:

The summary is your chance to tell your story. Highlight your career achievements, skills, and what makes you passionate about your field. Use a friendly, conversational tone.

Keep it concise but detailed enough to give a full picture of your professional journey.

---

[9]LinkedIn Photo Tips https://www.linkedin.com/business/talent/blog/product-tips/tips-for-taking-professional-linkedin-profile-pictures
[10] https://canva.com
[11] https:// www.remove.bg

Detailed Experience Section:

List both current and past positions. For each role, include specific responsibilities and accomplishments. Use action verbs and quantify results to showcase your impact.

Adding multimedia elements such as images, videos, or project links can make your experience stand out.

Skills and Endorsements:

List relevant skills that align with your career goals. Regularly updating this section is key as you acquire new skills.

Endorsements from colleagues enhance credibility. Don't hesitate to ask your network for endorsements, and offer to reciprocate.

Education and Certifications:

Include all formal education and relevant certifications or courses. This section is not just for degrees; include any ongoing professional development, workshops, or seminars.

Custom URL[12]:

A custom LinkedIn URL is more shareable and professional. Keep it simple, ideally just your name.

Recommendations:

Seek recommendations from a variety of people: supervisors, colleagues, subordinates. These testimonials add depth and authenticity to your profile.

---

[12] Customize Your LinkedIn URL:
https://www.linkedin.com/help/linkedin/answer/a542685

Volunteer Experience:

Showcasing your volunteer work demonstrates a well-rounded character. Include roles that might also highlight transferable skills relevant to your career.

Accomplishments and Projects:

This section is perfect for detailing significant achievements, awards, patents, or noteworthy projects that further illustrate your professional capabilities.

Active Engagement:

Consistently engage by sharing industry-relevant articles, insights, and participating in discussions. This keeps your profile active and visible in your network.

Profile Settings[13]:

Regularly review your privacy and visibility settings to ensure your profile is discoverable, especially by recruiters.

'Open To Work' Feature[14]:

Utilize the 'Open To Work' feature to indicate your availability to recruiters and your network. Be strategic about who you make this visible to.

Using AI for Crafting Content:

Employ AI tools to create engaging, professional content for your LinkedIn profile. Below are 30 AI prompts to assist in crafting an outstanding profile.

---

[13] LinkedIn Privacy Settings:
https://www.linkedin.com/mypreferences/d/categories/privacy
[14] Using LinkedIn Open To Work:
https://www.linkedin.com/help/linkedin/answer/a507508

Regular Updates:

Keep your profile dynamic and up-to-date, especially when actively seeking new opportunities.

Your LinkedIn profile is a dynamic tool in your professional toolkit. Beyond just showcasing your career history, it's a platform for establishing your professional brand, networking, and engaging with the broader industry community. A robust and active LinkedIn profile not only enhances your visibility to potential employers but positions you as an informed and engaged professional in your field.

Advanced Tips: Making Your Profile Stand Out Using AI Tools for Optimization

Once you've covered the basics of your LinkedIn profile, it's time to delve into advanced strategies to make your profile truly exceptional. Utilizing AI tools for optimization can give you a competitive edge. Here are some advanced tips and specific AI-driven prompts to enhance your LinkedIn presence.

Keyword Optimization Prompt: "Use AI to analyze the top 10 job descriptions for [Your Job Title] and identify common keywords to include in my LinkedIn profile."

Personal Branding Prompt: "Create a LinkedIn banner that embodies my personal brand as a [Your Profession], focusing on [Your Skills/Industry]."

Content Enhancement Prompt: "Improve my LinkedIn summary for clarity and impact, focusing on my achievements in [Your Field/Specific Project]."

Profile Analysis Prompt: "Analyze my LinkedIn profile against top profiles in [Your Industry] and suggest areas for improvement."

Optimal Posting Time Prompt: "Determine the best times for me to post on LinkedIn based on my network's engagement patterns."

Engagement Prediction Prompt: "Predict the engagement level for my LinkedIn article on [Your Article Topic]."

Networking Strategy Prompt: "Identify potential connections in [Your Industry] that align with my career goals of [Your Goals]."

Industry Trend Analysis Prompt: "Provide the latest trends in [Your Industry] to include in my LinkedIn posts."

Video Content Optimization Prompt: "Analyze engagement data for my LinkedIn video content and suggest themes that resonate with my audience."

LinkedIn Learning Path Recommendation: "Recommend LinkedIn Learning courses and paths that align with my career goals in [Your Job Title] or [Your Industry]."

Networking Event Analysis Prompt: "Identify upcoming networking events in [Your Industry] and prepare a strategy for effective networking and follow-ups."

Recommendation Strategy Prompt: "Suggest how to ask for and give effective LinkedIn recommendations to strengthen my profile."

Skill Gap Analysis Prompt: "Analyze the skill requirements for advanced roles in [Your Job Title] and recommend courses or certifications to bridge any gaps."

Content Series Development Prompt: "Develop a series of LinkedIn posts centered around [Your Expertise/Area of Interest], targeting audience engagement and thought leadership."

Profile Customization Prompt: "Suggest customizations for my LinkedIn profile to better appeal to recruiters in [Desired Industry/Role]."

Article Topic Generator Prompt: "Generate a list of compelling article topics that reflect current trends in [Your Industry]."

Group Engagement Strategy Prompt: "Propose strategies for engaging with and contributing to LinkedIn Groups related to [Your Profession/Interest]."

Endorsement Maximization Prompt: "Advise on how to effectively gain and give skill endorsements on LinkedIn."

Industry Influencer Identification Prompt: "Identify key influencers in [Your Industry] to follow and interact with for growing my professional network."

Volunteer Experience Showcase Prompt: "Suggest ways to effectively present my volunteer work and its relevance to my professional skills and aspirations."

Personalized Connection Requests Prompt: "Create templates for personalized connection requests that align with my career objectives."

Job Change Announcement Prompt: "Draft an engaging post to announce a new job or role change, highlighting my journey and future goals."

Project Showcase Prompt: "Guide me on how to effectively showcase a recent project or achievement in [Your Field] on my profile."

Profile Photo Optimization Prompt: "Recommend tips for choosing an impactful profile photo that aligns with my professional persona."

Career Milestone Celebration Prompt: "Suggest creative ways to celebrate and share career milestones on LinkedIn."

Alumni Networking Prompt: "Identify strategies for reconnecting and networking with college/university alumni in my field."

Webinar/Event Promotion Prompt: "Draft a post to effectively promote a webinar or event I'm hosting or participating in."

Feedback Request Strategy Prompt: "Develop a method for seeking constructive feedback on my projects or articles from my LinkedIn network."

Work Anniversary Post Prompt: "Compose a meaningful work anniversary post that reflects on my growth and future aspirations."

Diversity Advocacy Prompt: "Suggest ways to use my LinkedIn profile to advocate for diversity and inclusion in my workplace and industry

Utilizing these AI prompts, you can significantly elevate your LinkedIn profile, making it more compelling, relevant, and reflective of your professional persona. These tailored suggestions help in fine-tuning various aspects of your profile, ensuring it not only showcases your skills and experiences effectively but also resonates with your network and potential employers. Such an optimized LinkedIn profile serves as a robust tool in your networking and job search strategy, effectively highlighting your professional strengths and industry engagement.

Chapter 3: Resume and Cover Letter Mastery

Resume Writing: Step-by-step Guidance

Crafting a resume that stands out in today's job market requires a strategic approach. It's important to remember that there is no one-size-fits-all resume; each application should feature a resume tailored specifically to the job and the company. Your resume often serves as the first impression a potential employer has of you, making it essential to ensure it's impactful, concise, and aligned with the job you're applying for.

A customized resume should highlight the relevant skills and experiences that match the specific requirements of each job. This tailored approach demonstrates to employers that you possess not only the necessary qualifications but also a deep understanding of the role and how it fits within their organization.

Think of your resume as your value proposition to a potential employer. Based on my experience, investing a disproportionate amount of time on your resume is critical, as a well-crafted resume is a key factor in successfully securing employment. Additionally, always double-check for mistakes. Even a small error can lead to disqualification from the process, as it can negatively impact the professional impression you aim to convey.

Here's a step-by-step guide to creating an effective, customized resume:

Understanding the Purpose of Your Resume:

Your resume should succinctly showcase your skills, experience, and the value you can bring to a potential employer.

It's not just a list of past jobs; it's a tool to market yourself.

Choosing the Right Format:

Chronological: Best for those with a solid work history in the same field.

Functional: Focuses on skills and experience, suitable for career changers or those with gaps in their employment.

Combination: A blend of both, highlighting skills while providing a chronological work history.

Effective Structure and Content:

Header: Include your name, contact information, and professional LinkedIn profile or personal website.

Summary or Objective: A brief, compelling statement about your career goals and what you can offer.

Experience: List your work history, focusing on achievements rather than just duties. Use bullet points for clarity.

Education: Include degrees, certifications, and relevant training.

Skills: Highlight both hard (technical) and soft (interpersonal) skills.

Additional Sections: Consider adding volunteer work, publications, or projects if they enhance your candidacy.

Formatting Tips:

Keep it to one or two pages.

Use a clean, professional layout with easy-to-read fonts and adequate spacing.

Use bullet points to make information easily digestible.

Be consistent with your formatting choices (e.g., bullet style, date formats).

Customizing Your Resume:

Tailor your resume for each job application. Use the job description to identify and incorporate relevant keywords.

Highlight the experience and skills most relevant to each position.

Proofreading:

Check for grammar and spelling errors. Consider using tools like Grammarly or getting a friend to review it.

ATS Optimization:

Many companies use Applicant Tracking Systems (ATS) to screen resumes. Ensure your resume is ATS-friendly by using standard headings and avoiding graphics or unusual formatting.

ATS scans for specific keywords and phrases matching the job description and scores resumes based on the match.

Use clear, concise language, standard fonts, and avoid complex formatting.

Leveraging AI and Open-Source Tools:

Use AI tools like ChatGPT for feedback on your resume.

Open-source resources like Canva offer resume templates as a starting point.

Using these AI tools and ATS optimizers, job seekers can craft resumes that are not only professionally appealing but also tailored to pass through the filters of modern recruitment processes. These resources are invaluable in creating a resume that effectively showcases your skills and experiences in today's competitive job market.

Understanding and Optimizing for Applicant Tracking Systems (ATS):

ATS are software systems used by employers to filter resumes before they reach human eyes. They scan resumes for keywords, skills, previous employers, schools attended, and specific qualifications to determine if a candidate is a good match for the job.

How ATS Works:

Resumes are parsed and indexed into a database.

The system scans for specific keywords and phrases that match the job description.

Resumes are then scored based on how well they match the job criteria.

Optimization Tips:

Use keywords from the job description throughout your resume.

Stick to standard fonts and avoid complex formatting or graphics, as ATS may not read them correctly.

Use clear, concise language and avoid jargon or acronyms that might not be recognized by the ATS.

Examples of ATS-Friendly Resume Elements:

Standard headings like "Work Experience," "Education," and "Skills."

Bullet points with concise descriptions of duties and achievements.

Simple, straightforward language without overly complex sentence structures.

Utilizing AI Tools for Building and Optimizing Resumes

Several AI-powered tools can assist in creating a professional and visually appealing resume. Many of these tools offer free functionality, and some are specifically designed to ensure your resume is optimized for Applicant Tracking Systems (ATS). Here are some notable options:

Resume Genius[15]:

Offers a step-by-step guide for creating resumes, with a free trial available. It's user-friendly and ideal for those building a resume from scratch.

Zety[16]:

---

[15] https://resumegenius.com/
[16] https://zety.com/

Zety provides a free resume builder with tips and pre-written content to help get started, although full features require a subscription. It's useful for creating a professional-looking resume quickly.

Canva[17]:

Known for its design templates, Canva offers visually appealing and easily customizable resume templates for free, perfect for those looking to add a creative touch to their resumes.

Enhancv[18]:

Provides a basic free version for creating distinct and modern resumes. It's suitable for those who want to stand out with a unique resume design.

VisualCV[19]:

Offers a free tier with customizable templates and user-friendly editing tools, ideal for creating a professional CV or resume with ease.

Jobscan[20]:

Tailored for optimizing resumes against ATS, Jobscan offers compatibility scores and improvement suggestions by comparing your resume with job descriptions, crucial for tailoring your resume to specific job listings.

Resume Worded[21]:

[17] https://www.canva.com/
[18] https://enhancv.com/
[19] https://www.visualcv.com/
[20] https://www.jobscan.co/
[21] https://www.resumeworded.com/

This tool provides targeted feedback on resumes, evaluating them for ATS compatibility. It offers insights on keyword optimization and formatting, essential for making your resume stand out to both ATS and human recruiters.

Leveraging AI with Prompts for Resume Enhancement:

AI tools like ChatGPT can provide valuable assistance in refining your resume. Here are 30 prompts you can use:

Software Engineer Summary Development Prompt: "Craft a compelling professional summary for a software engineer with 5 years of experience, showcasing key projects and expertise [Insert specific projects and areas of expertise]."

Sales Manager Job Description Impact Enhancement Prompt: "Transform the phrase 'Worked as a sales manager' into a more dynamic and results-oriented job description [Insert specific responsibilities and achievements]."

Marketing Resume Action Verb Compilation Prompt: "Compile a list of dynamic action verbs tailored for a marketing professional's resume to amplify their accomplishments [Insert specific accomplishments for targeted verbs]."

Project Manager Achievement Quantification Prompt: "Provide examples of how to effectively quantify achievements for a project manager, focusing on project outcomes and leadership [Insert specific projects and leadership roles]."

Teamwork Skills Highlighting Prompt for Resumes: "Advise on articulating teamwork skills in a resume, demonstrating collaboration and interpersonal effectiveness [Insert specific teamwork experiences]."

Graphic Designer Experience Bullet Points Creation Prompt: "Develop a series of detailed bullet points for a graphic designer's experience section, emphasizing creative projects and design proficiency [Insert key projects and skills]."

Customer Service Representative Skills Identification Prompt: "List essential skills for a customer service representative, suitable for inclusion in their resume [Insert specific customer service roles and experiences]."

Resume Clarity and Conciseness Enhancement Prompt: "Critique and refine this resume excerpt [Insert resume excerpt], focusing on enhancing its clarity and succinctness."

Educational Leadership Experience Description Prompt: "Guide on how to articulate leadership experience in an educational role, highlighting key initiatives and leadership style [Insert specific leadership roles and initiatives]."

Finance Professional Resume Opening Line Prompt: "Compose an impactful and professional opening line for a finance professional's resume [Insert specific finance experience and skills]."

Cybersecurity Specialist Relevant Certifications Listing Prompt: "Identify and list certifications that are pertinent and advantageous for a cybersecurity specialist [Insert current certifications and desired career path]."

Resume Layout Optimization Prompt: "Offer suggestions to improve this resume's layout and design [Insert resume sample or layout description] for better readability and professional appeal."

Environmental Science Resume Tailoring Prompt: "Provide guidance on customizing a resume for a career in environmental science, focusing on relevant skills and experiences [Insert current resume content and desired job specifications]."

Skills Section Language Refinement Prompt: "Review and polish the language used in this resume's skills section [Insert skills section content], ensuring it's industry-relevant and impactful."

Engineering Career Objective Crafting Prompt: "Generate compelling career objective statements for engineers, aligning with industry advancements and personal growth goals [Insert specific engineering disciplines and career aspirations]."

Logistics Manager Industry Jargon Integration Prompt: "Identify and suggest key industry-specific jargon for inclusion in a logistics manager's resume [Insert current logistics experience and role]."

Remote Working Skills Showcase Prompt: "Advise on how to effectively highlight remote working skills and experience in a resume [Insert specific remote working experiences and skills]."

Freelance Project Description Composition Prompt: "Create an engaging and detailed description for a freelance project [Insert specific project details], showcasing project outcomes and skills applied."

Marketing Role International Experience Feature Prompt: "Suggest ways to effectively incorporate international experience into a resume for a marketing role [Insert specific international experiences and roles]."

Healthcare Cover Letter Introduction Improvement Prompt: "Enhance the introduction of this cover letter [Insert cover letter introduction] for a healthcare role to make it more engaging and relevant to the position."

Leadership Role Soft Skills Listing Prompt: "Generate a list of key soft skills suitable for a leadership role [Insert specific leadership experiences], tailored for inclusion in a professional profile."

Gap Year Presentation Strategy Prompt: "Advise on presenting a gap year on a resume in a way that highlights personal growth and professional development [Insert details about activities during the gap year]."

Biology Graduate Profile Summary Crafting Prompt: "Develop a compelling profile summary for a recent graduate in biology, emphasizing their academic background and research experience [Insert academic and research details]."

Extensive Work History Resume Formatting Tips Prompt: "Provide formatting tips for a resume with an extensive work history [Insert brief description of work history], ensuring it remains clear and easy to navigate."

Volunteer Work Integration in Resume Prompt: "Suggest effective ways to incorporate volunteer work into a resume, highlighting transferable skills and community involvement [Insert details of volunteer experiences]."

Retail Management Position Description Crafting Prompt: "Create a concise yet comprehensive job description for a retail management position [Insert specific management experiences], focusing on leadership and operational skills."

Digital Marketing Specialist Keywords Identification Prompt: "Identify key SEO-friendly keywords for a digital marketing specialist's resume [Insert current digital marketing skills and projects], enhancing its visibility and relevance."

Education Section Improvement Suggestions Prompt: "Review and provide suggestions for enhancing the education section of a resume [Insert current education section], focusing on relevance and academic accomplishments."

Technical Role Problem-Solving Skills Highlighting Prompt: "Suggest ways to effectively showcase problem-solving skills in a technical role [Insert specific technical experiences and challenges] on a resume."

HR Professional Summary Generation Prompt: "Develop an insightful summary section for a seasoned HR professional [Insert specific HR experience and goals], highlighting their experience and approach to human resources

By integrating these AI-generated insights and suggestions, you can significantly enhance the quality and effectiveness of your resume, making it more appealing to both ATS and human recruiters.

Cover Letter Creation: Tips for Writing Compelling Cover Letters That Complement Your Resume

Creating a strong cover letter is crucial for a successful job application. While it should complement your resume, it's equally important for the cover letter to address specific points from the job description. Bear in mind that not all recruiters require a cover letter; in fact, some may specifically prefer not to receive one. However, if the job application includes an option for a cover letter, it is advisable always to provide one.

Maintaining the right balance between length and content is key. As a former recruitment manager, I always valued cover letters that were short, consistent, and adequately comprehensive. A well-crafted cover letter should succinctly convey your qualifications and enthusiasm for the position, while also demonstrating your understanding of the job's requirements. Remember, a compelling cover letter can significantly enhance your application and set you apart from other candidates.

Here are key strategies:

Personalize Your Cover Letter:

Address the letter to the hiring manager or recruiter by name, if possible.

Tailor the content to the specific company and position.

Open Strongly:

Begin with a compelling opening line that grabs attention and clearly states your purpose.

Connect Your Skills to the Job:

Highlight the most relevant skills and experiences from your resume that are relevant to the job post.

Provide specific examples that demonstrate how your skills can benefit the company.

Show Your Enthusiasm:

Express genuine interest in the role and the company.

Explain why you're passionate about the opportunity.

Addressing Job Description Points:

Directly relate your experiences and skills to the requirements and responsibilities listed in the job description.

Close with a Call to Action:

End with a polite request for an interview or further discussion.

Thank the reader for their time and consideration.

Formatting and Length:

Keep the cover letter to one page.

Use a professional format and font, matching your resume style.

Proofread:

Check for errors in spelling, grammar, and punctuation.

Have someone else review it for clarity and impact.

Leveraging AI for Cover Letter Enhancement:

AI tools can assist in crafting and refining your cover letter. Here are 30 AI prompts for enhancing your cover letter:

Graphic Design Cover Letter Opening Line Prompt: "Craft an engaging opening line for a cover letter in the field of graphic design [Insert specific design achievements or passions], showcasing creativity and design passion."

Marketing Role Enthusiasm Expression Prompt: "Compose a statement expressing genuine enthusiasm for a marketing role [Insert personal marketing experiences or vision], highlighting personal drive and marketing vision."

Project Management in Construction Linkage Prompt: "Devise a way to effectively link project management skills to a role in construction [Insert specific project management experiences], focusing on coordination and oversight abilities."

Tech Startup Cover Letter Conclusion Prompt: "Create an impactful closing paragraph for a cover letter to a tech startup

[Insert personal innovation experiences or adaptability traits], emphasizing innovation and adaptability."

Sales Position Sentence Impact Enhancement Prompt: "Revise this sentence [Insert specific sentence from cover letter] to make it more compelling for a sales position, focusing on persuasion and results-driven language."

Managerial Role Leadership Highlight Prompt: "Generate a paragraph that accentuates leadership skills for a managerial role [Insert specific leadership experiences], underscoring team leadership and decision-making capabilities."

Teamwork in Nursing Cover Letter Mention Prompt: "Advise on incorporating teamwork skills in a cover letter for a nursing position [Insert specific teamwork experiences], reflecting collaborative patient care."

Company Culture Interest Expression in Cover Letter Prompt: "Formulate a statement showcasing interest in a company's culture for a cover letter [Insert personal values or experiences], aligning personal values with the company's ethos."

Customer Service Problem-Solving Story Prompt: "Create a narrative that demonstrates problem-solving skills in a customer service role [Insert a specific real-life example]."

Education Career Change Tailored Cover Letter Prompt: "Guide on tailoring a cover letter for someone transitioning into the education sector [Insert transferable skills and teaching passion], highlighting transferable skills and passion for teaching."

Recent Graduate Cover Letter Introduction Prompt: "Develop a compelling introduction for a recent graduate's cover letter [Insert academic achievements and enthusiasm], capturing fresh enthusiasm and academic achievements."

Linking Soft Skills to HR Role Example Prompt: "Provide an example of how to effectively incorporate soft skills in a cover letter for an HR position [Insert specific soft skills]."

Positive Gap Year Mention in Cover Letter Prompt: "Suggest a positive framing of a gap year in a cover letter [Insert gap year activities and skills learned], focusing on personal growth and acquired skills."

Adaptability Skills for Remote Job Paragraph Prompt: "Create a paragraph focusing on adaptability skills suitable for a cover letter applying to a remote job [Insert examples of adaptability in previous roles]."

Bilingual Skills Highlight in Cover Letter Prompt: "Advise on showcasing bilingual abilities in a cover letter [Insert specific languages and experiences], emphasizing the value in communication and cultural diversity."

Overcoming Challenges Professional Journey Discussion Prompt: "Guide on discussing overcoming professional challenges in a cover letter [Insert specific challenges and growth experiences], showing resilience and growth."

IT Career Switch Persuasive Argument Prompt: "Formulate a persuasive argument for a career switch into IT [Insert relevant skills and tech enthusiasm], highlighting relevant skills and tech enthusiasm."

Finance Role Interest Reaffirmation Conclusion Prompt: "Generate a concluding paragraph that reaffirms interest and suitability for a finance role [Insert personal finance skills and interests]."

Creativity Showcase in Advertising Cover Letter Prompt: "Provide examples of illustrating creativity in a cover letter for an advertising role [Insert innovative campaign ideas or experiences]."

Volunteer Experience in Non-Profit Cover Letter Mention Prompt: "Suggest ways to effectively mention volunteer experience in a cover letter for a non-profit role [Insert specific volunteer experiences and skills]."

Environmental Sustainability Passion Paragraph Prompt: "Create a paragraph expressing passion for environmental sustainability [Insert personal experiences or beliefs], suitable for a cover letter in a relevant field."

Incorporating Previous Job Feedback in Cover Letter Prompt: "Advise on how to include positive feedback from previous jobs in a cover letter [Insert specific examples of feedback], demonstrating professional growth."

International Experience Narrative in Cover Letter Prompt: "Develop a narrative that highlights international experience in a cover letter [Insert specific global experiences], showcasing global insights and adaptability."

Organizational Skills Highlight for Administrative Role Prompt: "Suggest how to emphasize organizational skills in a cover letter for an administrative position [Insert specific organizational experiences or achievements]."

Innovation Skills for R&D Position Paragraph Prompt: "Generate a paragraph that outlines innovation skills for a research and development role [Insert specific innovative projects or technical expertise], focusing on creativity and technical expertise."

Addressing Career Breaks in Cover Letter Prompt: "Advise on addressing career breaks due to personal reasons in a cover letter [Insert details about the break], turning them into positive learning experiences."

Hospitality Industry Cover Letter Opening Creation Prompt: "Craft an engaging opening for a cover letter in the hospitality industry [Insert customer service skills and industry passion], highlighting customer service skills and industry passion."

Continuous Learning Discussion in Cover Letter Prompt: "Suggest ways to effectively discuss commitment to continuous learning in a cover letter [Insert examples of continuous learning or development]."

Awards and Recognitions Mention in Cover Letter Prompt: "Provide a compelling way to mention awards or recognitions in a cover letter [Insert specific awards or recognitions], demonstrating excellence and dedication."

Confident and Hopeful Cover Letter Conclusion Prompt: "Generate a strategy for concluding a cover letter on a note of confidence and optimism [Insert personal strengths or aspirations], looking forward to the opportunity for an interview.

Using these AI prompts, you can enhance your cover letter, making it more personalized, engaging, and aligned with the job you're applying for. This approach ensures that your cover letter complements your resume, effectively conveying your suitability and enthusiasm for the role.

Chapter 4: Evaluating Job Opportunities

This chapter presents a systematic approach to assess if a job opportunity aligns with your skills, experience, and career goals, integrating AI tools to refine the process. A critical aspect of job searching is to thoughtfully and wisely invest your time. It's essential to rigorously evaluate each opportunity; if a job doesn't meet your criteria or if you lack the required competencies, it's advisable not to apply.

Reflecting on my personal job search journey, I learned a valuable lesson. Initially, I sent out as many resumes as possible, attempting to cast a wide net. Unfortunately, this approach often led to no responses from many applications. The crucial strategy is to focus your efforts on opportunities that align closely with your profile and aspirations. By doing this, you not only save time but also increase your chances of securing a job that truly suits you.

The critical step is understanding your current skills and competencies and comparing them against the job post requirements. An effective method is to list your skills and then meticulously go through the job post, identifying requirements stated explicitly or implied. Matching your abilities with the expectations for a successful candidate is key. Equally important is honesty in self-assessment. The tools and strategies outlined below can assist in self-evaluation, gap analysis (which can be addressed before an interview, for example), and aligning your skills and expectations with job requirements and company profiles.

A profound understanding of your skills, competencies, and abilities in relation to your potential employer's requirements and expectations is crucial for successful recruitment and your future career with that employer. An initial step I recommend is to evaluate the company's values and see how they align with your own. For instance, if you prefer working independently and the company heavily emphasizes teamwork, applying for that job might not be the best choice.

Let's now review the tools, applications, and AI prompts that can help you understand your position, gauge future employer expectations, and decide whether to respond to a given opportunity.

Skills and Experience Compatibility:

Self-Assessment[22]: Engage in a thorough self-assessment of your skills by utilizing resources like LinkedIn Skills Assesment. These tools not only validate your existing skills but also pinpoint areas where you can improve. Regularly engaging in these assessments ensures you are up-to-date with the competencies required in your field.

Job Description Analysis[23]: Leverage AI-powered tools such as jobscan to meticulously compare your resume with job descriptions. This analysis is crucial in identifying how well your skills and experiences align with the requirements of the job, ensuring that you present yourself as the ideal candidate for the role.

Gap Analysis: Actively use educational platforms like Coursera[24] or Udemy[25] to conduct a detailed gap analysis. These sites offer a wide array of courses designed to help you bridge any skills gaps you might have. They provide an opportunity for continuous learning and staying competitive in your field.

Alignment with Career Goals:

Career Trajectory Analysis: Utilize insightful career exploration tools like CareerExplorer[26] or CareerFitter[27] These resources offer comprehensive support in assessing how a particular job aligns with

---

[22] LinkedIn's Skill Assessments: https://www.linkedin.com/skill-assessments/hub/quizzes/

[23] https://www.jobscan.co/

[24] https://www.coursera.org/

[25] https://www.udemy.com/

[26] https://www.careerexplorer.com/

[27] https://www.careerfitter.com/

your long-term career goals, helping you to chart a clear and strategic path forward in your professional journey.

Learning Opportunities: Conduct thorough research into a company's commitment to employee development. Platforms like Glassdoor are invaluable for uncovering insights about a company's training programs and growth opportunities. This research is key in finding a workplace that supports and enhances your professional development.

Industry Relevance: Maintain an active presence in LinkedIn groups and industry-specific forums. Staying informed about the latest trends, demands, and conversations in your industry is essential for ensuring your skills and knowledge remain relevant and cutting-edge.

Evaluating Company Culture and Values:

Company Research: Deeply explore a company's culture, mission, and values using LinkedIn and Glassdoor. This research is crucial in understanding the ethos of the company and determining if it aligns with your personal values and professional ethos.

Employee Feedback: Read through employee reviews on platforms like Glassdoor to gain insights into the company's work environment and management style. These reviews can offer a candid glimpse into the day-to-day realities of working at the company.

Network Insights: Harness the power of your LinkedIn network to connect with current or former employees. Gaining firsthand experiences and insights from these connections can provide invaluable context that goes beyond what is publicly available.

Work-Life Balance Consideration:

Job Demands: Utilize tools like Timely[28] to meticulously track and analyze work hours and demands in roles similar to what you are considering. This information helps you understand the time

---

[28] https://timelyapp.com/

commitment and workload you can expect, allowing you to gauge if it aligns with your work-life balance goals.

Personal Life Impact: Reflect critically on how the role complements or conflicts with your personal life priorities and commitments. It's essential to find a position that harmonically integrates with your lifestyle and personal responsibilities.

Compensation and Benefits Evaluation:

Market Comparison: Use comprehensive tools like Payscale[29] and Salary.com[30] to gather data for market salary comparisons. This step is crucial in ensuring that you are adequately compensated according to industry standards and regional cost of living.

Personal Needs: Assess the benefits package offered in light of your personal financial goals and needs. This assessment should consider aspects like health insurance, retirement plans, and other perks that align with your long-term financial planning. Future Prospects and Stability:

Company Stability: Investigate the company's financial health, especially if it's publicly traded, using platforms like Yahoo Finance[31]. Understanding a company's financial status can offer insights into its stability and longevity in the market.

Future Growth: Engage with industry reports and market analysis tools to evaluate the company's potential for future growth and innovation. This research is key in ensuring that the company not only has a solid present but also a promising future in an ever-evolving business landscape.

By utilizing these strategies and AI tools, you can conduct a thorough and informed evaluation of job opportunities. This approach ensures

---

[29] https://www.payscale.com/en-eu/
[30] https://www.salary.com/
[31] https://finance.yahoo.com/

that the roles you pursue align not only with your professional skills and career aspirations but also with your personal values and life goals. Making well-informed decisions in your job search is crucial in finding a role that is not just a job, but a stepping stone in your career journey.

30 AI Promp   to Support Job Opportunity Evaluation:

Evaluate the job post skills and competencies Prompt:

„Evaluate the following job post and provide a list of the required skills and competencies. Analyze the wording of the post and identify key qualifications, skills, and experience the employer is looking for. Here is the job post:

[Insert Job Post Text Here]

Based on this job post, please list out:

Essential Skills and Competencies: Identify and list the skills and competencies explicitly stated as essential in the job post.

Desirable Skills and Competencies: Note any skills and competencies that are mentioned as desirable or advantageous for the candidate to have.

Implied Skills and Competencies: If there are any skills or competencies that are not explicitly mentioned but implied or suggested as important due to the nature of the job or responsibilities, please list them as well.

Experience Requirements: Detail any specific experience required or preferred, as mentioned in the job post."

Company Culture Assessment Questions Prompt: "List insightful questions to ask in an interview [Insert specific role or company] to gauge a company's culture and values."

Work-Life Balance Factors in Tech Role Analysis Prompt: "Identify key factors to consider when evaluating work-life balance in a technology role [Insert specific role details]."

AI-Assisted Company Growth Research Prompt: "Guide on using AI tools [Specify AI tools] to research and assess a company's [Insert company name] growth prospects and financial stability."

Healthcare Job Benefits Evaluation Checklist Prompt: "Create a comprehensive checklist for assessing the benefits offered in a healthcare position [Insert job title and company]."

Marketing Job Offers Comparison Assistance Prompt: "Provide a framework to compare two job offers in the marketing field [Insert details of offers], considering key aspects like salary, benefits, and career growth."

Finance Role Career Advancement Query Generation Prompt: "Develop a set of questions [Insert specific finance role] to inquire about career advancement opportunities in a finance role."

Engineering Job Market Trend Analysis via AI Prompt: "Advise on utilizing AI tools [Specify AI tools] to analyze current job market trends and opportunities in the engineering sector [Insert specific engineering field]."

LinkedIn AI Feature Utilization for Job Search Tips Prompt: "Offer practical tips for leveraging LinkedIn's AI-driven features [Specify features] to optimize job search efforts [Insert job search goals]."

Remote Work Opportunities Assessment Template Prompt: "Formulate a template for evaluating the suitability and benefits of remote work opportunities [Insert specific job titles or companies]."

Startup Environment Suitability Evaluation Prompt: "Create a guide to help assess how well a startup environment [Insert specific startup] aligns with personal career goals and work style."

Retail Company Career Path Insights Generation Prompt: "Generate insights on various career paths within a retail company [Insert company name], including growth and development opportunities."

Leadership Team Evaluation Methods Prompt: "Suggest effective methods for evaluating the leadership team of a potential employer [Insert employer name], focusing on their track record and leadership style."

Company Stability Assessment Guide Prompt: "Develop a guide to assess the stability of a company [Insert company name] in the current economic climate, considering factors like market position and financial health."

Impact of Company Size on Career Development Analysis Prompt: "Advise on how to analyze the impact of a company's size

[Insert company name] on individual career development and opportunities."

Tech Company Innovation Culture Assessment Criteria Prompt: "Create criteria for evaluating the innovation culture of a tech company [Insert company name], focusing on creativity and technological advancement."

International Job Opportunities Comparison Template Prompt: "Provide a template for comparing job opportunities in different countries [Insert countries or job titles], taking into account cultural, legal, and economic factors."

Employee Testimonial Evaluation on Company Review Sites Prompt: "Suggest ways to evaluate employee testimonials on company review sites [Insert specific sites] for genuine insights into the company culture [Insert company name]."

Diversity and Inclusion Practices Assessment Checklist Prompt: "Create a checklist to assess a company's [Insert company name] diversity and inclusion practices in the workplace."

AI-Driven Red Flag Identification in Job Listings Prompt: "Guide on how to use AI tools [Specify AI tools] to identify potential red flags in job listings [Insert job listing details], such as unrealistic requirements or vague descriptions."

Training and Development Quality Assessment Guide Prompt: "Develop a guide for evaluating the quality and effectiveness of a company's [Insert company name] training and development programs."

Company Competitive Positioning Analysis Prompt: "Suggest ways to analyze a company's [Insert company name] competitive positioning in its industry, considering factors like market share and innovation."

High-Growth Startup Risk and Reward Evaluation Framework Prompt: "Create a framework for evaluating the risks and rewards associated with joining a high-growth startup [Insert startup name]."

Long-Term Career Impact of Job Switch Assessment Prompt: "Advise on how to assess the long-term career impact of switching jobs [Insert current and potential job titles], considering factors like career trajectory and skill development."

Company Sustainability and Social Responsibility Evaluation Criteria Prompt: "Generate criteria for evaluating a company's [Insert company name] commitment to sustainability and social responsibility."

Sector-Wise Compensation Package Comparison Method Prompt: "Provide a method for comparing compensation packages across different sectors [Insert sectors], including benefits and perks."

AI-Enhanced Emerging Job Trends Identification Prompt: "Suggest ways to use AI tools [Specify AI tools] to identify emerging job trends in a specific field or industry [Insert field or industry]."

Job Security Assessment Strategy in Fluctuating Market Prompt: "Develop a strategy for assessing job security and stability in a fluctuating market environment [Insert specific job market or industry]."

Job Role and Personal Values Alignment Evaluation Prompt: "Guide on evaluating the alignment of a job role [Insert job title] with personal values and ethics."

Creative Expression Opportunities in Job Assessment Guide

Prompt:

"Generate a guide for assessing opportunities for creative expression and innovation in a job role [Insert job title]."

These prompts are designed to help job seekers use AI tools effectively to analyze and evaluate various aspects of job opportunities, ensuring a good fit with their career aspirations and personal preferences.

Chapter 5: Enhanced Interview Preparation Strategies

Congratulations on reaching this critical stage of the job search process. Now, the real excitement begins. Interviews are an essential step where you get the chance to showcase your skills, experience, and how well you fit the role. In this chapter, I'll classify different types of interviews and outline strategies for effective preparation. Remember, no two interviews, interviewers, or processes are the same. Each interview is a unique event that demands specific preparation.

A general rule is to gather as much information as possible about the company and the individuals interviewing you. A good starting point is the company's website, social media platforms, search engines, and AI-driven research tools. I recall an interview with a VP of Sales where I used Google to find articles she had written and videos of her discussing sales strategies. During the interview, I aligned my responses closely with her insights and philosophy, which worked exceptionally well.

Research, preparation, and practice are the pillars of successful interview preparation. Don't enter this crucial phase in your path to employment without thorough preparation. The effort you've put in to reach this point must now be leveraged to its fullest. Also, remember that adequate preparation can significantly reduce stress and increase your comfort level during the interview. Different types of interviews require specific preparation strategies, which we will explore in detail in the following sections.

Types of Interviews:

Traditional Interviews: Focus on experiences, skills, and cultural fit. Prepare to discuss your resume and how your experiences align with the job.

Behavioral Interviews: Centered around how you've handled past situations. Use the STAR Method[32] to structure your responses.

Technical Interviews: Common in STEM fields, focusing on technical skills and problem-solving. Review key industry concepts and prepare to demonstrate your expertise.

Panel Interviews: Involve multiple interviewers. Engage with each person, and be prepared to address questions from different perspectives.

Video Interviews: Require technical setup in addition to interview preparation. Ensure good lighting, a stable internet connection, and a quiet environment.

What to Expect:

Preparation: Conduct thorough research on the company and role. Understand the company's mission, culture, and how they align with your career objectives.

Common Themes: Be ready to discuss your professional background, problem-solving abilities, and career aspirations.

Interactive Elements: Prepare for potential role-specific tasks or assessments.

---

[32] https://www.themuse.com/advice/star-interview-method

AI-Powered Mock Interviews:

Using AI Tools:

ChatGPT and Similar Platforms: Practice with AI interview simulations. Platforms like Interviewing.io[33] offer real-life interview scenarios with AI.

Customizable Scenarios: Tailor your practice sessions to the job or industry you're targeting.

Feedback: AI tools can critique your answers for clarity and relevance, aiding improvement.

Question Predictions:

AI Analysis: Use tools like LeetCode[34] for tech interviews or VMock[35] for general interview preparation to get predicted questions.

Industry-Specific Queries: AI can help understand the common questions for specific roles or industries, allowing for targeted preparation.

Answering Interview Questions:

Effective Responses:

STAR Method: An effective way to answer behavioral questions. Learn about STAR Method.

Relevance: Align your responses with the job description and company values.

Clarity and Conciseness: Practice delivering clear, concise answers.

---

[33] https://interviewing.io/
[34] https://leetcode.com/
[35] https://www.vmock.com/

Common Interview Questions:

Strengths and Weaknesses: Prepare strategic responses that show self-awareness. Common Interview Questions[36]

Past Experiences: Highlight achievements relevant to the role.

Career Goals: Discuss your aspirations and how they align with the company's future.

This chapter equips job seekers with targeted strategies for different types of interviews. Leveraging AI for practice, along with understanding the format and expectations of each interview type, can significantly enhance your preparedness and confidence. Remember, the key to a successful interview is a combination of thorough research, strategic preparation, and the ability to articulate your experiences and skills effectively.

Here are 30 sophisticated AI prompts that job seekers can use to prepare for interviews:

Prompt to Gather Information about an Interviewer:

---

[36] Common Interview questions list by Indeed: https://www.indeed.com/career-advice/interviewing/top-interview-questions-and-answers

"ChatGPT, I have a job interview coming up and I need to gather some specific information about the person who will be interviewing me. The interviewer's name is [Insert Interviewer's Name]. Please help me find the following details:

Professional Background:

What is their current role at the company?

Can you provide a brief overview of their career path and key professional achievements?

Educational Background:

What is their educational background, including the institutions they attended and any notable degrees or qualifications?

Publications or Media Appearances:

Have they written any articles, books, or papers?

Are there any interviews, podcasts, or public speaking events they have participated in?

Social Media Profiles:

Can you find their LinkedIn profile or other professional social media presence?

Are there any insights into their professional interests or recent activities?

Personal Interests (if publicly available):

Are there any hobbies or interests they have mentioned in a professional context?

Company Involvement:

What has been their role or contribution in major projects or initiatives at the company?

Interview Style (if information is available):

Is there any information available on their interviewing style or common questions they ask?

Project Management Tight Deadlines Handling Prompt: "Simulate a challenging interview question on managing tight deadlines in a project management role [Insert specific project type], focusing on time management and prioritization skills."

Tech Startup Innovation Discussion Scenario Prompt: "Create a scenario for an interview that discusses bringing innovation to a tech startup [Insert startup specifics], emphasizing creative thinking and adaptability."

Teamwork in High-Pressure Environment Behavioral Question Prompt: "Generate a behavioral interview question about working in a team under high pressure [Insert specific industry or project], focusing on collaboration and stress management."

Colleague Conflict Handling Question Prompt: "Simulate an interview question that explores handling conflicts with colleagues [Insert specific work scenario], emphasizing communication skills and emotional intelligence."

Significant Marketing Achievement Discussion Scenario Prompt: "Create a scenario for discussing a significant marketing achievement [Insert specific campaign or project], focusing on strategy implementation and results measurement."

Engineering Technical Problem-Solving Question Prompt: "Develop a technical question for an engineering interview [Insert specific engineering field], focusing on problem-solving abilities and technical knowledge application."

Customer Service Challenges Situational Question Prompt: "Propose a situational interview question about handling customer service challenges [Insert specific service scenario], focusing on customer empathy and resolution skills."

Managerial Position Leadership Scenario Prompt: "Simulate a leadership scenario for a managerial position [Insert specific management level], focusing on team leadership and decision-making abilities."

Creativity and Efficiency Balance in Design Question Prompt: "Create an interview question about balancing creativity and efficiency in design roles [Insert specific design field], emphasizing time management and creative output."

Decision-Making Under Uncertainty Scenario Prompt: "Generate a scenario that explores decision-making under uncertainty [Insert specific business context], highlighting analytical thinking and risk assessment."

IT Role New Technologies Integration Question Prompt: "Formulate a question about integrating new technologies in an IT role [Insert specific IT area], focusing on tech adaptability and innovation."

Diversity Management in Workplace Question Prompt: "Propose an interview question on managing diversity in the workplace [Insert specific industry], highlighting inclusivity and cultural awareness."

Personal Growth from Past Failures Discussion Scenario Prompt: "Create a scenario for discussing personal growth from past failures [Insert specific past experience], emphasizing resilience and learning from experience."

Long-Term Career Planning in Finance Question Prompt: "Simulate a question about long-term career planning in finance [Insert specific finance role], focusing on career goals and industry trends."

Legal Profession Ethical Dilemma Scenario Prompt: "Generate an ethical dilemma scenario relevant to legal professions [Insert specific legal context], focusing on ethical judgment and problem-solving."

Business Development Strategic Planning Question Prompt: "Create a challenging question about strategic planning in business development [Insert specific business area], emphasizing vision and strategic thinking."

Corporate Sustainability Initiatives Discussion Scenario Prompt: "Develop a scenario discussing involvement in sustainability initiatives in a corporate setting [Insert specific corporate context], highlighting environmental awareness and initiative."

Dynamic Market Sales Strategy Adaptation Question Prompt: "Formulate a question about adapting sales strategies in a dynamic market [Insert specific market], focusing on market analysis and flexibility."

Difficult Consulting Client Situation Prompt: "Simulate a situation dealing with a difficult client in consulting [Insert specific client scenario], focusing on client management and conflict resolution."

Team Leadership Through Organizational Change Question Prompt: "Create an interview question about leading a team through organizational change [Insert specific change scenario], emphasizing leadership and adaptability."

Data Leveraging in Decision-Making Processes Question Prompt: "Generate a question on leveraging data in decision-making processes [Insert specific decision context], highlighting analytical skills and data interpretation."

Effective Communication in Remote Teams Scenario Prompt: "Propose a scenario about effective communication in remote teams [Insert specific remote work context], focusing on communication tools and team cohesion."

Positive Work Culture Fostering Question Prompt: "Simulate a question on fostering a positive work culture [Insert specific company or team], emphasizing leadership style and team engagement."

Project Budget Constraints Handling Scenario Prompt: "Create a scenario about handling budget constraints in a project [Insert specific project type], focusing on financial management and resource optimization."

Industry Trends Update Staying Question Prompt: "Develop a question about staying updated with industry trends [Insert specific industry], highlighting commitment to professional development and industry awareness."

Busy Schedule Task Prioritization Situational Question Prompt: "Formulate a situational question about prioritizing tasks in a busy schedule [Insert specific job role], focusing on time management and prioritization skills."

Collaborative Project Contributions Question Prompt: "Simulate a question about contributions to a collaborative project [Insert specific project details], emphasizing teamwork and project management."

Competitive Market Navigation Challenging Scenario Prompt: "Create a challenging scenario about navigating a competitive market [Insert specific market], focusing on strategic thinking and market analysis."

Professional Challenges Resilience Discussion Prompt: "Generate a question discussing resilience in facing professional challenges [Insert specific challenge context], highlighting perseverance and adaptive problem-solving.

These prompts cover a wide range of scenarios and topics, helping job seekers to prepare comprehensively for various types of interview questions and discussions.

Chapter 6: Salary Negotiation and Benefits

Reaching this stage in your job search journey suggests that you are close to a successful hire. However, there are various scenarios to consider, especially regarding salary. Increasingly, job descriptions are listing salary or salary ranges, and sometimes recruiters or hiring managers mention potential salaries early in the process. Let me share some personal experiences to illustrate this.

In one instance, I successfully negotiated an offer that was 23% above the initial budget for the position. Conversely, I have also declined discussions where the initial salary offer was significantly below my expectations. While there's no one-size-fits-all rule, a general guideline I recommend is to always ask for more or, at the very least, express that you had anticipated a better offer.

An exception to this rule can occur in hiring processes for lower-skilled positions, where the recruiting team might choose the most cost-effective candidate among similarly qualified applicants. However, this is not a frequent occurrence. Remember, if you don't ask, you won't get an answer. It sounds straightforward, but it's a crucial point that's easy to overlook. I've experienced this firsthand; in the excitement of being offered a job, I once forgot about this fundamental strategy.

Let me also mention an important note: more and more companies are offering additional benefits like stock options, car allowances, gym memberships, meal reimbursements, and, notably, commissions. These perks are significant, especially as commissions can constitute a substantial portion of your income in sales roles. However, based on my experience, the base salary is paramount, particularly in challenging times. For instance, severance pay, if you are let go, or compensation during sickness, in many jurisdictions, is based on your base salary. So, while these perks are attractive, what truly matters is the base salary, and for sales positions, the commission component.

In this chapter, I will guide you through tools and techniques to better prepare for salary negotiations. These strategies will empower you to approach this crucial phase of the job search process with confidence and knowledge.

Unlock the Power of Your Worth: Arm yourself with knowledge of the market's pulse. Dive into resources like Payscale and Glassdoor to unearth the standard rates for your role across various locales.

Acknowledge the worth of your unique blend of skills, experiences, and accomplishments. Discover your market value here.

Strategize Your Desires: Chart out your salary and benefits wishlist, prioritizing them to anchor your negotiation talks around what fuels your passion and meets your needs.

Collaborative Guidance: Transform negotiation into a two-way street by inviting the hiring manager to share their insights post-presentation of your case. It's not just about demands; it's about reaching common ground.

Choosing Your Arena: Whether it's the formality of emails or the spontaneity of calls, choose the medium that resonates with your communication style.

The Art of Attentive Listening: Tune in to the undertones of the hiring manager's responses. Their words hold the key to aligning your aspirations with the company's vision.

The Power of a Pause: Use silence as your strategic ally. A pause, post-offer, can often lead to the table turning in your favor.

Engage with Curiosity: Counter resistance with curiosity. Open-ended questions can peel back the layers of any constraints, nurturing a solution-focused dialogue.

The Dance of Counteroffers: Don't shy away from the counteroffer waltz. A 'no' is just the prelude to your negotiation symphony.

Positive Persuasion: Keep the negotiation narrative affirmative. Ultimatums can backfire, but positivity paves the path to agreement.

Beyond the Paycheck: Widen the lens to see beyond the salary. Benefits such as work-life harmony, time off, or a title upgrade can be golden.

Persistence Pays: Hone your negotiation craft; with every dialogue, you're not just shaping your current package but also sculpting your future as a negotiation maestro.

AI as Your Negotiation Scout: Harness the analytical prowess of AI. Tools like Payscale and Glassdoor not only offer you a glimpse into competitive salaries but also arm you with data-centric tactics tailored to your professional narrative.

For a deeper dive into advanced negotiation techniques, including psychological tactics and scenario planning, explore the following free resources:

Alison Free Online Negotiation Courses[37]: Offers a range of courses teaching skills to build relationships and reach beneficial outcomes in negotiations.

The Muse: How to Negotiate Salary[38]: How to Negotiate Salary: Offers guidance and strategies specifically tailored for salary negotiations, including tips on how to approach the conversation and what factors to consider.

Coursera: How to Negotiate Salary[39]: How to Negotiate Salary: Features a structured course or set of lessons that delve into salary negotiation tactics, offering insights and techniques to help individuals effectively negotiate their salaries.

Forbes: How to Negotiate a Winning Salary[40]: How to Negotiate a Winning Salary: Presents expert advice and strategies from a reputable source, focusing on how to successfully negotiate a salary that reflects one's value and meets their career goals.

---

[37] https://alison.com/tag/negotiation

[38] https://www.themuse.com/advice/how-to-negotiate-salary-37-tips-you-need-to-know

[39] https://www.coursera.org/articles/how-to-negotiate-salary

[40] https://www.forbes.com/sites/forbescoachescouncil/2022/04/25/how-to-negotiate-a-winning-salary/

Robert Half: 8 Tips for Salary Negotiations[41]: 8 Tips for Salary Negotiations: Provides a concise list of eight practical tips for salary negotiations, aimed at helping individuals prepare and execute a successful salary negotiation strategy.

30 AI Prompts for Salary Negotiation Preparation

Mid-Level Marketing Manager Salary Negotiation Simulation Prompt: "Simulate a salary negotiation conversation for a mid-level marketing manager [Insert specific achievements and market value], focusing on achievements and market value."

Health Benefits Inquiry List During Salary Negotiation Prompt: "Generate a comprehensive list of questions [Insert specific benefit queries] to inquire about health benefits during salary negotiations."

Data Analysis Skills-Based Salary Increase Scenario Prompt: "Create a scenario for negotiating a higher salary [Insert specific data analysis skills and achievements] based on unique skills and achievements in data analysis."

Remote Work Options Negotiation Dialogue Example Prompt: "Provide a dialogue example [Insert specific remote work preferences] showcasing how to negotiate remote work options effectively."

---

[41] https://www.roberthalf.com/us/en/insights/career-development/be-ready-for-salary-negotiations-with-these-8-tips

Software Developer Lowball Salary Offer Response Simulation Prompt: "Simulate a professional and assertive response [Insert response details] to an initial lowball salary offer for a software developer position."

Performance-Based Bonuses in Sales Discussion Prompt: "Create a prompt for a discussion [Insert specific performance metrics] on negotiating performance-based bonuses in sales roles."

Education Reimbursement Package Negotiation Strategy Prompt: "Formulate a negotiation strategy [Insert specific educational goals] for obtaining a higher education reimbursement package."

Additional Vacation Time Negotiation Tactics Prompt: "Suggest practical ways [Insert desired vacation time] to negotiate additional vacation time in a job offer discussion."

Signing Bonus Negotiation Scenario Prompt: "Provide a realistic scenario [Insert expected bonus amount] for negotiating a signing bonus during a job offer discussion."

Customer Service Role Flexible Hours Discussion Prompt: "Generate a dialogue [Insert desired flexible hours] focusing on negotiating flexible working hours in a customer service role."

Post-Probation Period Salary Increase Negotiation Prompt: "Create a prompt [Insert expected salary increase] for negotiating a salary increase after successfully completing a probation period."

Startup Equity or Stock Options Negotiation Dialogue Simulation Prompt: "Simulate a conversation [Insert desired equity or stock options] for negotiating equity or stock options in a startup environment."

Relocation Package Negotiation Scenario Prompt: "Devise a scenario [Insert relocation needs] for negotiating a comprehensive relocation package with a potential employer."

Cost of Living Adjustment Salary Discussion Strategy Prompt: "Develop a strategy [Insert specific cost of living factors] for discussing a salary adjustment based on cost of living increases."

Health Insurance Plan Details Clarification Questions Prompt: "Suggest targeted questions [Insert specific coverage queries] to clarify the details and coverage of a health insurance plan during negotiations."

Negotiating a Better Title for Same Salary Offer Prompt: "Formulate a prompt [Insert desired title] for negotiating a more prestigious title while maintaining the same salary offer."

Responding to Minimum Range Salary Offer Simulation Prompt: "Simulate a professional response [Insert counteroffer details] to a salary offer that meets the minimum but not the ideal range."

Salary Terms Review Request Dialogue Generation Prompt: "Generate a dialogue [Insert specific terms for review] for professionally requesting a review of salary terms after a year of employment."

Presenting Market Research in Salary Negotiation Prompt: "Advise on how to effectively present market research data [Insert specific market data] during salary negotiations to justify a higher offer."

Professional Development Opportunities Negotiation Scenario Prompt: "Create a scenario [Insert specific development opportunities] for negotiating additional opportunities for professional development during a job offer discussion."

Flexible Spending Account Negotiation Conversation Prompt: "Develop a conversation [Insert specific FSA benefits] focusing on negotiating a flexible spending account as part of a benefits package."

Retirement Plan Options Discussion Strategy Prompt: "Provide a strategy [Insert desired retirement plan options] for discussing and negotiating favorable retirement plan options."

Annual Travel Stipend Negotiation Simulation Prompt: "Simulate a negotiation scenario [Insert stipend expectations] for obtaining an annual travel stipend as part of a job offer."

Maternity/Paternity Leave Policy Discussion Prompt: "Formulate a prompt [Insert specific leave policy queries] for discussing and understanding a company's maternity/paternity leave policies."

Telecommuting Options Negotiation Scenario Prompt: "Generate a realistic scenario [Insert specific telecommuting needs] for negotiating telecommuting options, emphasizing work-life balance."

Addressing Salary Cap Limitations in Negotiation Prompt: "Suggest effective ways [Insert potential negotiation strategies] to address and navigate salary cap limitations during salary negotiations."

Non-Monetary Benefits Counteroffer Strategy Prompt: "Create a strategy [Insert desired non-monetary benefits] for countering a salary offer with a request for non-monetary benefits, such as additional leave or flexible hours."

Negotiating a Later Start Date Dialogue Prompt: "Devise a dialogue [Insert preferred start date] for negotiating a later start date that accommodates personal circumstances or commitments."

Bonus Eligibility Criteria Discussion Scenario Prompt: "Provide a scenario [Insert specific bonus criteria] for discussing and understanding the criteria for bonus eligibility during job negotiations."

Early Performance Review for Salary Reassessment Conversation Prompt: "Simulate a conversation [Insert specific review timing and salary reassessment goals] for negotiating an early performance review with the possibility of salary reassessment

These prompts cover a range of scenarios and considerations, equipping job seekers with the tools and confidence needed to effectively navigate salary and benefits negotiations.

Chapter 7: Using AI and Open-Source Tools Effectively

In the ever-evolving landscape of job hunting, AI and open-source tools stand out as powerful allies. This chapter delves into how these technologies can significantly enhance your job search and application process. My journey has been enriched by the strategic use of these tools, offering insights and practical examples to help you navigate this terrain.

One vivid example from my own experience is the innovative use of ChatGPT for cover letter preparation. By feeding my CV and the job description into the AI, and asking it to craft a cover letter of a specific length, I was able to create personalized and highly relevant applications. This approach not only saved time but also ensured that my cover letters were sharply aligned with both my professional profile and the job requirements. I'm quoting this prompt below.

This chapter will explore a variety of AI and open-source tools, each offering unique advantages in different aspects of the job search. From optimizing your resume to networking effectively, these tools can provide a competitive edge. We'll look at how to select the right tools for your needs, use them to their full potential, and integrate them seamlessly into your job search strategy.

Embrace the journey through this chapter as a pathway to mastering these modern tools, enhancing your job search, and stepping confidently into your next professional adventure.

Overview of AI Tools for Job Hunting:

ChatGPT by OpenAI[42]: A versatile AI chatbot that can assist with crafting resumes, cover letters, and interview responses. Users can practice mock interviews, get career advice, and even receive help in writing professional emails and LinkedIn messages.

Bing AI[43]: Microsoft's search engine with integrated AI capabilities, ideal for comprehensive research on companies, industry trends, and specific job roles. It also offers job seekers valuable insights into the current job market and potential career paths.

Google's Bard[44]: An AI tool from Google, still in development, expected to provide job seekers with tailored advice, up-to-date job market information, and industry-specific preparation tips. It aims to help users understand complex job roles and refine their job search strategies.

LinkedIn AI Features: Leveraging AI, LinkedIn offers personalized job recommendations based on your profile and past activity. It also provides tools for resume optimization and interview preparation, making it easier to connect with potential employers.

AI Job Search Engines: Platforms like Indeed and Monster[45] use AI algorithms to match candidates with job listings that align with their skills and preferences, streamlining the job search process.

---

[42] https://openai.com/chatgpt
[43] https://www.bing.com/
[44] https://bard.google.com/chat
[45] https://www.monster.com/

AI Resume Writers: Tools like Kickresume[46], Rezi[47], and Skillroads[48] utilize AI, including GPT-4 in some cases, to create tailored resumes. They offer suggestions for bullet points, summaries, and skills based on job titles, making resume creation more efficient and effective.

AI Job Matching Platforms: Platforms such as Talentprise[49], Pyjama Jobs[50], and Fortay[51] use AI to match job seekers with opportunities that fit their skills, experience, and preferred company culture, including remote positions. These platforms are especially useful for personalized job searches.

Applicant Tracking Systems (ATS) Optimization Tools: Tools like Jobscan[52] are designed to help job seekers optimize their resumes to pass through ATS filters used by many companies, ensuring higher visibility for their applications.

Open-Source CV Tools

Canva[53]: Offers a wide array of free, visually appealing resume templates that are easy to customize, suitable for job seekers looking to create professional and eye-catching resumes.

Google Docs Resume Templates[54]: Provides a variety of free, simple, and easy-to-use resume templates, accessible with a Google account, ideal for quick resume creation and editing.

---

[46] https://www.kickresume.com/en/

[47] https://www.rezi.ai/

[48] https://skillroads.com/

[49] https://www.talentprise.com/

[50] https://www.kickresume.com/en/

[51] https://fortay.co/

[52] https://www.jobscan.co/

[53] https://www.canva.com/

[54] https://docs.google.com/document/u/0/?ftv=1&tgif=d

GitHub Resume Generator[55]: A unique tool for tech professionals, this generator creates a resume based on a user's GitHub profile, showcasing their projects and coding experience effectively.

LaTeX Resume Templates on Overleaf[56]: For those who prefer precision formatting, Overleaf offers numerous LaTeX resume templates, allowing for the creation of professionally formatted and typeset documents.

Portfolio Websites: GitHub Pages[57] and GitLab[58] offer free hosting for personal portfolio websites, allowing job seekers, especially those in creative and technical fields, to showcase their work alongside their CVs.

Glassdoor: Provides invaluable insights into company cultures, salaries, and interview processes, helping job seekers tailor their applications and prepare for interviews with specific companies. Glassdoor.

Each of these tools offers unique advantages to job seekers, helping them navigate the complexities of the job market more effectively and increasing their chances of landing their desired roles.

Prompt for AI to Write a Cover Letter:

"Hello ChatGPT, I need your assistance in writing a cover letter for a job application. Below, I have pasted my resume and the job description for the position I am applying for. Please use this information to create a tailored cover letter that effectively highlights my relevant skills and experiences in relation to the job requirements. The cover letter should be [specify length, e.g., one page long].

My Resume: [Paste the content of your resume here]

---

[55] https://resume.github.io/
[56] https://www.overleaf.com/gallery/tagged/cv
[57] https://pages.github.com/
[58] https://about.gitlab.com/stages-devops-lifecycle/pages/

Job Description: [Paste the job description here]

Based on the above information, please write a cover letter that includes the following elements:

An introduction that expresses my interest in the position.

A brief overview of my most relevant skills and experiences, specifically aligned with the requirements of the job.

Mention of any specific achievements or projects from my resume that are particularly relevant to the job.

A closing paragraph that reiterates my enthusiasm for the role and invites further discussion or an intervie"

Chapter 8: Maximizing Networking in Your Job Search

In my view, networking is the most crucial aspect of the job search process, especially as you aim for higher positions. Reflecting on my own career trajectory, nearly every job transition I've made, except for my very first role post-graduation, involved an insider's reference or a personal referral. This underscores the vital importance of building and maintaining genuine, positive relationships in both your personal and professional life. Focusing on solutions, helping others, staying energetic, and being ready to take on new tasks are key components of successful relationship building.

While the art of building relationships could itself be the subject of an entire book, consider this a critical piece of advice for your future endeavors. The focus of this chapter, however, is on how to effectively leverage the relationships you have already built. We will explore how to approach your network in a systematic manner, aiming to utilize these connections to your advantage in the job search process. This chapter is designed to guide you through the strategic use of your network, enhancing your job search and opening doors to new opportunities.

Leveraging Relationships in the Job Seeking Process

Networking plays a crucial role in the job search process. It's not just about who you know, but also how you engage with your network to uncover opportunities. Here's a step-by-step guide on how to effectively leverage your personal and professional relationships:

Creating a Comprehensive Contact List:

Compile a list of all the people you know who could potentially assist in your job search. Use LinkedIn, Facebook, Instagram, and other networks to jog your memory.

Don't limit yourself to just professional contacts; include friends, family, and acquaintances.

Developing a Networking Scorecard:

In a spreadsheet, list the names of your contacts.

Influence Score (1-10): Rate each contact based on their influence or position (e.g., a CEO might be rated higher than a junior employee).

Relationship Strength (1-10): Assess the strength of your relationship with each contact (consider frequency of interaction, closeness, etc.).

Total Networking Score: Add the Influence and Relationship scores. This will help prioritize contacts with the highest potential to assist in your job search.

Contacting Your Network:

Personalized Approach: Tailor your communication based on your relationship strength. For closer contacts, a direct and personal approach works best.

Professional Etiquette: For more distant contacts, maintain professionalism. A LinkedIn message or a formal email may be more appropriate.

Request for Assistance: Clearly state your job search goals. Ask if they're aware of any opportunities or if they can introduce you to someone who might.

Networking Events and Meetups:

Attend industry events, conferences, and meetups. These are excellent opportunities to expand your network.

Prepare an elevator pitch about your skills and the kind of opportunities you're seeking.

Follow-Up and Gratitude:

Always follow up with a thank you note or message expressing gratitude for any assistance received.

Keep your contacts informed about your job search progress.

Expanding Your Network:

Join professional groups and forums related to your field.

Engage with content on platforms like LinkedIn to increase your visibility.

Maintaining Relationships:

Networking is a two-way street. Offer help and support to your contacts where you can.

Stay in touch even after your job search is over to maintain and strengthen these relationships.

By strategically leveraging your network, you not only increase your chances of finding job opportunities but also build a support system that can be invaluable throughout your career. Remember, networking is about building genuine connections and mutually beneficial relationships.

Here's an list of 30 AI prompts to enhance the networking process for job seekers:

Former Colleague Reconnection on LinkedIn Prompt: "Compose a personalized message for reconnecting with a former colleague on LinkedIn [Insert colleague's name], inquiring about job opportunities and sharing recent career updates [Insert personal updates]."

Tech Industry Networking Event Icebreakers Prompt: "List engaging icebreaker questions [Insert specific topics or interests] tailored for networking events in the tech industry, facilitating meaningful conversations."

Professional Contact Referral Email Template Prompt: "Develop a template for an email [Insert specific referral request] politely asking for a job referral from a professional contact, highlighting mutual benefits."

Finance Professional Elevator Pitch Development Prompt: "Craft a brief yet compelling elevator pitch for a finance professional [Insert specific achievements and skills] seeking new opportunities, focusing on key achievements and skills."

Career Advice Phone Call Script with a Mentor Prompt: "Provide a script for a phone call to a mentor [Insert mentor's name], discussing career aspirations, seeking advice, and inquiring about potential leads [Insert specific questions]."

LinkedIn Job Search Announcement Post Prompt: "Generate a professional yet engaging LinkedIn post [Insert post content] to announce your job search to your network, inviting leads and opportunities."

Second-Degree LinkedIn Connection Outreach Template Prompt: "Create a message template [Insert message content] for reaching out to a second-degree connection on LinkedIn, requesting an informational interview [Insert interview goals]."

Follow-Up Message After Unresponded Job Inquiry Prompt: "Suggest a polite and effective follow-up message [Insert follow-up content] for a contact who hasn't responded to a previous job inquiry."

Informational Interview Questions Series Prompt: "Develop a series of insightful questions [Insert specific questions] to ask during an informational interview with a professional in your desired industry."

Job Lead Thank-You Message Generation Prompt: "Generate a gracious thank-you message [Insert thank-you note content] for a contact who provided a job lead or introduction, expressing appreciation and interest."

Industry Leaders Networking Message at Conference Prompt: "Compose a networking message [Insert message content] to engage with industry leaders at a conference, introducing yourself and expressing interest in their work."

University Alumni Job Search Advice Email Draft Prompt: "Draft an email [Insert email content] to a university alumnus asking for job search advice and insights in their field, highlighting your shared background."

Post-Networking Event Follow-Up Message Prompt: "Create a follow-up message [Insert follow-up content] after a networking event to continue the conversation, expressing interest in future collaborations."

Virtual Networking Session Conversation Starters Prompt: "Suggest conversation starters [Insert specific topics] tailored for a virtual networking session, facilitating engaging and relevant discussions."

LinkedIn Recommendation Request from Supervisor Prompt: "Generate a polite request [Insert request content] for a LinkedIn recommendation from a previous supervisor, emphasizing your professional growth and collaboration."

Old Classmates Professional Networking Message Prompt: "Develop a message [Insert message content] for reconnecting with old classmates on professional networks, sharing updates and exploring mutual interests."

Job Lead Response Crafting Prompt: "Craft a professional and enthusiastic response [Insert response content] to a job lead shared by a contact, expressing interest and gratitude."

Part-Time/Freelance Opportunities Inquiry Prompt: "Compose an inquiry message [Insert inquiry content] for part-time or freelance opportunities within your professional network, highlighting your relevant skills and flexibility."

Network Introduction Request Script Prompt: "Create a script [Insert script content] for politely asking a contact to introduce you to someone in their network, emphasizing the mutual benefit of the connection."

Coffee Chat Invitation for Potential Mentor Prompt: "Draft an inviting message [Insert invitation content] for a coffee chat with a potential mentor, expressing admiration for their work and desire for guidance."

LinkedIn Professional Achievement Update Prompt: "Generate a LinkedIn status update [Insert update content] to share a recent professional achievement, engaging your network and showcasing your progress."

Message to Former Professor for Industry Insights Prompt: "Suggest a respectful message [Insert message content] to a former professor, inquiring about industry insights and potential job leads in their field of expertise."

Outreach Email to Potential Employer via Contact Prompt: "Create a professional outreach email [Insert email content] to a potential employer spotted through a contact's network, expressing interest in the company and seeking further information."

Insight-Seeking Message for Company Insider Prompt: "Draft a message [Insert message content] to a contact working at a company you're interested in, seeking insights and advice on potential opportunities."

Declining a Job Offer via Networking Contact Prompt: "Develop a polite and concise message [Insert message content] for declining a job offer through a networking contact, maintaining a positive relationship."

Professional Development Update Email to Network Prompt: "Compose an email [Insert email content] updating your network on recent professional development activities or certifications, showcasing your commitment to growth."

Resume Feedback Request Message Prompt: "Generate a message [Insert request details] requesting constructive feedback on your resume from trusted contacts in your network."

Industry Change Advice Request Note Prompt: "Craft a note [Insert note content] asking for advice on transitioning to a different industry, addressed to a contact experienced in that field."

Recruiter Re-engagement LinkedIn Message Prompt: "Formulate a LinkedIn message [Insert message content] to re-engage with a recruiter previously met at a job fair, highlighting your recent professional advancements."

Volunteer Opportunities Inquiry Email in Industry Prompt: "Create an email [Insert email content] seeking volunteer opportunities in your industry, aiming to expand your network and gain additional experience.

These AI prompts provide a diverse range of scenarios, helping job seekers to effectively utilize their networks, maintain professional relationships, and seek new opportunities in their job search journey.

Chapter 9: Maintaining a Log of Your Job Seeking Activities

In the multifaceted journey of job seeking, one often overlooked yet crucial aspect is the management of a detailed log of your activities. This chapter delves into the significance and practical methods of maintaining such a log, emphasizing its role not just in tracking your efforts but also in enhancing your interactions with potential employers and connections.

Keeping a log of your job-seeking activities does more than just record the positions you've applied for or the interviews you've attended. It serves as a repository of valuable details and interactions that can be pivotal in future engagements. Imagine being able to impress a potential employer or a network contact by recalling specific details from a conversation that happened weeks or even months ago. Such attentiveness to detail demonstrates your dedication and thorough approach, traits highly valued in any professional setting.

Furthermore, this log can help you analyze patterns in your job search, identify strategies that are working, and refine those that aren't. It becomes a tool for self-reflection and continuous improvement, guiding you towards more targeted and effective job-seeking strategies.

In this chapter, we will explore the best practices for maintaining this log, including what information to record, how to organize it effectively, and how to utilize it to your advantage in your job search. By the end of this chapter, you will appreciate the power of a well-maintained job-seeking log as an integral part of your job search toolkit.

Importance of Tracking Your Job Search

In the journey of job searching, staying organized is key. Keeping a detailed log of your job-seeking activities not only helps you manage your applications effectively but also allows you to analyze your efforts and strategize accordingly. This chapter provides comprehensive guidance on how to maintain an effective job search log.

Setting Up Your Job Search Log:

Choose a Format: Decide whether you prefer a digital tool like a spreadsheet (Google Sheets or Microsoft Excel) or a physical notebook. Digital tools offer more flexibility and searchability.

Structure: Your log should include columns for the job title, company, date applied, job description (link if online), resume and cover letter versions used, contact method, contact person (if available), follow-up dates, comments, and status updates.

Logging Applications:

Job Description and Link: Always save a copy of the job description. If it's an online listing, save the link or a PDF of the page.

Resume and Cover Letter Versions: Note which version of your resume and cover letter you used. This helps in keeping track of customizations for each application.

Date and Method of Application: Record the date you applied and whether it was through an online portal, email, or another method.

Tracking Communications:

Contacts and Responses: Log any communication with company representatives, including names, dates, and key points discussed.

Interviews and Meetings: Keep detailed notes about interviews or informal meetings, including date, time, platform (in-person, video call, etc.), and interviewers' names.

Follow-Up Actions:

Reminders: Set reminders for follow-ups or thank-you notes post-application or interview.

Status Updates: Regularly update the log with any responses received, additional communications, or changes in the application status.

Review and Analysis:

Periodic Review: Regularly review your job search log to assess your activity patterns, response rates, and any areas needing improvement.

Strategic Adjustments: Use insights from your log to refine your job search strategy. Identify which types of roles, industries, or companies are yielding better responses.

Benefits of a Job Search Log:

Organization: Keeps your job search efforts organized and manageable.

Accountability: Helps in maintaining a consistent job search routine.

Insightful: Provides valuable insights into the effectiveness of your job search strategies.

Tools and Resources:

Google Sheets/Excel Templates: Utilize templates available online specifically designed for job search tracking.

Job Search Apps: Consider using job search apps or software that offer built-in tracking and organization features.

By diligently maintaining a log of your job-seeking activities, you gain greater control over your job search process. This organized approach not only ensures that no opportunity slips through the cracks but also empowers you to make data-driven decisions about your job search strategies. Remember, in job searching, as in many areas of life, the details matter. Keeping a thorough record is a small effort that can yield significant.

Conclusion

Final Thoughts

As we conclude this guide, it's important to reflect on the key takeaways from each chapter. The journey of job hunting in the digital age is dynamic and requires an adaptable approach. From understanding the evolving job market to leveraging AI and open-source `tools, every step is crucial in paving the way toward your ideal career.

Adaptability and Continuous Learning: Embrace the rapidly changing job landscape and commit to ongoing learning and skill development.

AI and Technology Utilization: Leverage AI tools for resume building, interview preparation, and job market research to stay ahead in the competitive job market.

Networking: Utilize your personal and professional networks effectively, understanding that relationships can often open doors to opportunities that are not visible on job boards.

Strategic Job Application: Tailor your applications, from your resume to cover letters, using AI tools and open-source resources to enhance their impact.

Interview Preparedness: Practice and prepare for interviews using AI mock interviews and familiarize yourself with different interview formats.

Salary Negotiation: Approach salary negotiation with confidence, armed with research and a clear understanding of your worth.

Holistic Approach: Remember, job hunting is not just about finding any job; it's about finding the right job that aligns with your career goals, skills, and personal values.

Embarking on a job search can be a challenging but rewarding journey. With the right tools, resources, and approach, you can navigate this path successfully. Remember, every step you take is a learning experience that brings you closer to your career goals. Stay persistent, adaptable, and proactive. Your dream job awaits!

In "Your Path to Employment," we have explored the dynamic and evolving world of job hunting, leveraging the power of AI and open-source tools. This guide has provided you with an extensive array of strategies and insights for navigating today's job market, emphasizing the importance of resilience and adaptability. The essence of your job search success lies in persistence, preparation, and proactivity. As you implement these principles and the techniques from this book, remember that challenges are stepping stones to your goals. Your journey might be demanding, but it is within these moments that opportunities are seized and careers are shaped. Good luck on your path to employment, and remember, true luck often arises from a blend of preparation, persistence, and proactivity. May this guide be your steadfast companion in achieving the career success you seek and deserve.

As we reach the conclusion of this journey together, I want to extend my deepest gratitude to you, the reader. Your commitment to navigating the pages of this book is not just a testament to your dedication to personal and professional growth, but also a source of immense inspiration for me.

If you found value in the insights and strategies shared in this book, I kindly encourage you to share your experience with others. One of the most impactful ways you can do this is by leaving a review on Amazon. Your feedback not only helps me to improve and evolve, but more importantly, it serves as a valuable guide for future readers who are on their own path to employment.

Your reviews and thoughts are incredibly meaningful, not just to me as the author but to the wider community seeking guidance and inspiration in their career journey. So, if you have a moment, please head over to Amazon and share your thoughts. Your voice can make a significant difference and be a beacon of support for others.

Thank you once again for being a part of this journey. Here's to your continued success and the countless achievements that await you in your career path.

Rafal Laba

Appendix

Your thoughts and feedback are invaluable to us. If you have suggestions, questions, or would like to share your experience with the book, please feel free to reach out at rafal@rafallaba.pl. Your insights will greatly contribute to future editions and help us better cater to your job-seeking needs. Thank you for joining us on this journey towards successful employment.

Additional Resources:

To further aid your job search, here are additional resources, including open-source tools and websites:

LinkedIn Learning[59]: Offers a wide range of courses for skill development and career advice.

Coursera[60]: Access courses on various subjects to enhance your professional knowledge.

Indeed Career Guide[61]: Provides tips and advice on all aspects of job searching.

Harvard Business Review[62]: A wealth of articles on career development and management skills.

Meetup[63]: Find and join professional networking groups and events in your area.

TED Talks[64]: Inspirational talks that can provide motivation and new perspectives on career growth.

Khan Academy[65]: Free resources for learning new skills and personal development.

---

[59] https://www.linkedin.com/learning/

[60] https://www.coursera.org/

[61] https://www.indeed.com/career-advice

[62] https://hbr.org/

[63] https://www.meetup.com/

[64] https://www.ted.com/topics/career

[65] https://www.khanacademy.org/

Frequently Asked Questions

1. **How effective are AI tools in enhancing job applications?** AI tools can significantly improve job applications by offering personalized suggestions, optimizing for keywords, and enhancing the overall presentation of your resume and cover letter.

2. **Can AI help with interview preparation?** Yes, AI can assist in interview preparation by providing mock interview scenarios, feedback on responses, and helping you formulate answers to common interview questions.

3. **What's the best way to use LinkedIn for job searching?** Optimize your profile with relevant keywords, actively network with industry professionals, engage with content, and utilize LinkedIn's job search feature.

4. **How often should I update my resume?** Update your resume regularly, especially when you gain new skills, experiences, or certifications. Keeping your resume current ensures you're always ready for unexpected opportunities.

5. **Is it necessary to tailor my resume for each job application?** Yes, tailoring your resume for each application

increases your chances of passing through Applicant Tracking Systems (ATS) and appealing to the specific needs of the employer.

6. **How can I use Glassdoor effectively in my job search?** Use Glassdoor to research company cultures, salary ranges, and employee reviews, and to prepare for interviews by reading about other candidates' experiences.

7. **What are the best open-source tools for resume building?** Canva, Google Docs Resume Templates, and LaTeX Templates on Overleaf are excellent for creating professional and visually appealing resumes.

8. **How important is networking in the job search process?** Networking is crucial as it can uncover hidden job opportunities, provide industry insights, and increase your chances of referral.

9. **Can AI tools help in salary negotiation?** AI tools can provide market salary data and help you simulate negotiation scenarios, preparing you for real discussions.

10. **What should I do if I'm not getting responses to my job applications?** Consider revising your resume, seek feedback, and broaden your job search strategy to include networking and targeting companies directly.

11. **How can social media platforms other than LinkedIn contribute to job search efforts?** Platforms like Twitter and Facebook can be used to follow industry news, connect with professionals, and discover job postings in informal settings.

12. **Are online career fairs effective for job searching?** Yes, online career fairs offer a unique opportunity to network with

multiple employers, learn about various industries, and potentially secure interviews.

13. **What role do personal projects or portfolios play in the job search?** Personal projects and portfolios can significantly enhance your application by showcasing your skills, creativity, and commitment to your field.

14. **How can I leverage volunteer experience in my job search?** Volunteer experience can be a valuable addition to your resume, demonstrating your initiative, skills, and commitment to community service.

15. **What strategies can I use to stay motivated during a prolonged job search?** Set achievable goals, maintain a routine, seek support from peers or mentors, and celebrate small victories to stay motivated.

16. **How can I effectively research a company before applying?** Utilize resources like the company website, press releases, and industry reports to gain insights into the company's culture, values, and recent developments.

17. **What are the advantages of using job search apps on mobile devices?** Job search apps offer convenience, real-time alerts, and the ability to apply to jobs quickly, making it easier to stay engaged with your job search on the go.

18. **How do I handle gaps in my employment history?** Be honest about employment gaps, focus on skills and experiences gained during those periods, and articulate how these have prepared you for your next role.

19. **Is it beneficial to work with a career coach or counselor?** A career coach or counselor can provide personalized advice, help refine your job search strategy, and offer support and guidance through the job search process.

20. **What are effective strategies for remote job searching?** Tailor your application to highlight skills relevant to remote work, utilize remote-specific job boards, and demonstrate your ability to work independently and manage time effectively.

These FAQs and the glossary provide a quick reference to some of the most common questions and terms related to job searching and the use of AI tools, helping you navigate your job search journey with more confidence and understanding.

Glossary

Terms to Know

1. AI (Artificial Intelligence): **Technology that simulates human intelligence processes through algorithms and machine learning.**
2. Applicant Tracking System (ATS): **Software used by companies to filter resumes and manage the hiring process.**
3. Behavioral Interview: **An interviewing technique that focuses on a candidate's past experiences and behaviors.**
4. Elevator Pitch: **A brief, persuasive speech used to spark interest in what you or your organization does.**
5. LinkedIn: **A social networking platform geared towards professionals and job seekers.**
6. Mock Interview: **A practice interview to prepare a job seeker for the real interview experience.**
7. Networking: **The process of interacting with others to exchange information and develop professional or social contacts.**

8. Open-Source Tools: **Software tools that are freely available for use and modification, often used for resume building and job searching.**
9. Portfolio: **A collection of work samples that demonstrate your skills and qualifications.**
10. Remote Work: **A work arrangement in which employees do not commute to a central place of work.**
11. Soft Skills: **Personal attributes that enable someone to interact effectively and harmoniously with other people.**
12. Cover Letter: **A document sent with your resume to provide additional information on your skills and experience.**
13. Career Fair: **An event where employers and recruiters meet with potential employees.**
14. Freelancing: **Working as an independent contractor rather than being employed by someone else.**
15. Glassdoor: **A website where current and former employees anonymously review companies and their management.**
16. Headhunter: **A recruiter who seeks out candidates, often for senior positions.**
17. Job Board: **A website that posts job openings submitted by employers.**
18. Personal Branding: **The practice of marketing oneself and their careers as brands.**
19. Recruiter: **An individual who works to fill job openings in businesses or organizations.**

20. Salary Negotiation: **The process of discussing and arriving at a mutual agreement regarding an employee's pay.**